Missouri
on my mind

FALCON PRESS

Design, typesetting, and other prepress work
by Falcon Press, Helena, Montana.
Printed in Japan.

Library of Congress Number: 90-55233

ISBN 1-56044-045-7

Front cover photos
Alley Spring Mill near Eminence
Bald eagle along the Mississippi River

Back cover photos
Pony Express Statue in St. Joseph
Fall colors in the Ozarks
Tom and Becky look-alikes in Hannibal
Wheat in northeast Missouri

All cover photos by Frank Oberle

For extra copies of this book
Please check with your local bookstore, or write to
Falcon Press, P.O. Box 1718, Helena, MT 59624.
You also may call toll-free 1-800-582-BOOK.

Missouri woods near old Monroe squeeze the last light of day   FRANK OBERLE

introduction

Sometimes in the twilight of an Ozark evening, I hear ghosts talking. They're the spirits of dead Missourians, and they know I'm an admirer. So they take me into their confidence. They drift whispering around the porch of the old cabin where I come to watch the setting sun turn creeks and fields to amber. The cabin is at least a century old. Some of the ghosts are older than that.

I'm at that cabin now, watching the glory being born. Ozark sunsets are among the most splendid in the world, and I've been all over the world to compare, from Sri Lanka to Spain. None of them can hold a candle to the fiery eruptions that drip from an after-storm Missouri sky like scarlet paint thrown against a canvas.

The spirits sigh restlessly among the oaks and cedars. *Come on, come on,* they say. *We left our beds to be with you. Come on. . . .*

I rise, for I must not let them down. I love these pioneer dead as I love my adopted state of Missouri. I'll go with them for awhile and read the books of their lives in upright stone pages. Then we'll stroll together among the woods and flowers, catching a final late breeze, watching the velvet robes of night chase the last golden auras from the fields.

I wasn't born in Missouri, but neither were the ancestors of those who were born here. Pioneers from many places, they adopted, as I did, a new land and a new life.

And pioneers are what Missouri is all about—not disinfected heroes on pedestals with shaded eyes looking west, but the disenfranchised and disenchanted from other lands and other times. They were Mormons recruited from England, Catholics and Jews from Europe, Buddhists from the Far East. Some were so desperate for a new and better life that they were willing to die for it. Persecuted Mormons died with their handcarts on the plains. Despairing Cherokees followed their Trail of Tears. Jesse James, abandoned by his gold-seeking father, turned to his gun for consolation. Starving street urchins from New York rode the Orphan Trains to Missouri in the early 1900s, hoping to find loving families.

They came, settled or pushed on, lived or died, and Missouri is greater for them all. Determined dreamers on a hard frontier, they lived by sweat, cunning, and guns. Blood was often shed, but teachers came, and preachers, too. Slowly civilization arrived.

The ghosts drifting like gossamer around me understand what that civilization cost. Some of them were there. They were marketers, or mayors, or pirates, or gamblers on riverboats. Some were politicians, river rascals, prostitutes—subjects of paintings by such artists as George Caleb Bingham, whose home in Arrow Rock, a tiny restored historical village, still stands.

Missouri is saturated with history. Hernando de Soto, Francisco de Coronado, and Daniel Boone trod the green, haze-filled

Tiger swallowtail decorating a spike of blazing star FRANK OBERLE

valleys and climbed the rocky hills. Boone is buried near his last home, Defiance, thirty-four miles from St. Louis. Kit Carson ran away from bondage in New Franklin, where the Santa Fe Trail originated. Jesse James ended his days in St. Joseph, where the Pony Express was born.

Missouri is synonymous with great names: Harry S Truman (whose middle initial bore no period), George Washington Carver, Joseph Pulitzer, Dale Carnegie, Omar Bradley, Laura Ingalls Wilder, T.S. Eliot, and Thomas Hart Benton are just a few who called the state home.

Missouri's rivers, the Mississippi and the Missouri chief among them, loom large in the history of the state and the nation. Lewis and Clark began and ended their great expedition at a dock in St. Louis. A 630-foot stainless steel arch, the Jefferson National Expansion Memorial, now stands near the site. Known more commonly as the Gateway Arch, it attracts two million visitors a year. Perhaps some of them, like me, fancy they hear the ghostly voice of Thomas Jefferson praising this monument to his dream of westward expansion.

I hear ghostly voices, too, when I stroll in the evening along the Big Muddy, as the Missouri is called. I hear the leadsman's voice drifting reedlike on the wind: "Quarter less twaaiinnn! Maaarrkk Twaainn!" Samuel Clemens, Missouri's most famous native, adopted the cry and penned many of his works under the name Mark Twain. North of St. Louis on the Mississippi, Twain's hometown of Hannibal keeps his

memory alive with various events. I've stood below the bronze statues of Tom and Huck, watched whitewash fly during fence-painting contests, and visited nearby Rennselaer and the grave of Becky Thatcher. Her name was Laura Hawkins Frazer in real life—and I wondered how one book could bring such fame to a simple village girl. I've also stood in the shrine that protects Mark Twain's tiny two-room birthplace near Florida, Missouri, and imagined the shouts of 1830s urchins at play.

There's no monotony in Missouri. It has landscapes some say could only have been dreamed. These include Graniteville's Elephant Rocks—igneous boulders the size and shape of pachyderms. More than a billion years old, they're the gift of volcanic activity and eons of erosion.

Missouri is also a land of chert—what archaeologists call flint and what Indians used to make arrowheads. These are still found almost routinely, plowed up or washed up on riverbanks. The mineral, durable and harder than glass, also was used to pave many early Missouri highways. Jasper, agate, and mozarkite (Missouri's official state rock) are other cherty rocks, some of them cantaloupe-sized and shaped, found especially near Osceola. And "Carthage marble" from Carthage once was shipped around the world.

Missouri place names sometimes confound visitors. Who would name a camp, later a town, Rocky Comfort? Is Peculiar, Missouri, really peculiar? And where but in Missouri could a person visit Mexico, Cuba, California, Nevada, Paris, and Beverly Hills without leaving the state?

When I think of Missouri, though, I most often think of the vast 55,000-square-mile Ozark Plateau. Why not, when two-thirds of the state lies within this tangled range? Eons ago, the Ozarks may have arched as high as the Himalayas, but time has ground them down like an old mule's teeth. Today the highest peak in Missouri is 1,772-foot Taum Sauk, near Ironton.

When I drive the lonely, two-lane mountain

Lake of the Ozarks   FRANK OBERLE

highways, past hamlets or wide spots in the road, peering down sheer cliffs or up at towering bluffs, I revel in what has been lost to most Americans—the slow, enjoyable sipping of sights and sounds. From Springfield in the southwest to St. Louis in the east, the Ozarks are a tumbled land of gorges, limestone bluffs, bright rivers, and more caves (seven thousand known; more being discovered) than any other place in the world. Rolling farmland, emerald green, takes over where crags leave off. And the forests—well, the daddy of them all is the Mark Twain National Forest, which blankets the state from below St. Louis to Roaring River in the southwest. I've roamed there and camped there and seen wild turkeys and deer, more abundant now than in 1900, thanks to the state Department of Conservation.

Spring finds the hills tapestried with dogwoods, while the pastures are Pointillists' canvases of wildflowers—goldenrod, verbena, Sweet William, and wild roses. The endless humming of millions of bees sounds like a distant angels' choir.

Free-flowing waterways and hundred-mile trails lure canoeists and backpackers who, unaware, follow routes used by old stagecoaches or early-day fur trappers. Beavers, foxes, badgers, and woodchucks are still plentiful. Missouri is also known for its gigantic freshwater springs. Big Spring, in the southeastern part of the state, is America's largest single-outlet spring. On an average day, it gushes forth some 277 million gallons of pure fresh water.

Water-rich Missouri offers a wide range of fish, but two are unique: the gar and the paddlefish. The latter, with its spatula nose, is a bottom feeder that exists in the Ozarks and only a few other places on earth. Gar are needle-mouthed fish with iron-hard scales. The largest on record reached nine feet and weighed 301 pounds. Both fish date to prehistoric times, but I don't fish for them. I fish for bass, and I remember one superb day when I, a lousy fisherman,

caught a fine four-pounder while an expert from a big tackle company only caught chiggers. Fishing luck runs both ways.

I love hiking and biking and once bicycled across Missouri in October. The skies saw fit to drown me for four of the five days it took. The bike I used, now six years old, glares at me as if to say, "Don't get any dumb ideas—I don't do odysseys anymore." Missouri has trails for any feet or seat and invites anyone to tramp through its fallen leaves or damp grasses. Recently another section of the Katy Trail opened near the old railroad town of Rocheport, on abandoned railbeds donated by the M-K-T Railroad. When it's completed, perhaps by 1993, it will stretch two hundred miles along rivers and past towering bluffs bright with water and wildflowers. An even larger, more historic trail starts below St. Louis and ends in Oklahoma: the four-hundred-mile-plus Ozark Trail, which follows the old Butterfield Stagecoach route.

In the southwestern Missouri Ozarks, where my parents still live on a small farm, towns look old and crumbly. Visitors see them as moribund or dying, which is exactly what we want them to see. Ozarkians aren't greatly concerned with the world outside, and one man who died at 106 had never strayed more than a few miles from his home. Folks here like it quiet enough to talk to God, which they often do.

The rugged, up-and-down topography of Missouri makes for an interesting climate. When it comes to weather, the state is an enigma perched on a riddle. I've glanced out my window one moment and seen Noah's ark float past, and just minutes later I've watched

Fall-colored woods near Hannibal FRANK OBERLE

birds drying off in the sun. Weather forecasters are rarely right for long.

Two years of drouth recently ended, quite properly, with a deluge that lasted for days. Up came the rivers and out came the canoes and john boats. Still, this flood will have to go some to beat the summer of 1844, when the Missouri River crested in St. Louis at thirty-eight feet, seven inches—still a record. But today, locks, dams, and levees have tamed the river considerably, the better for it to carry enormous amounts of barge freight.

Mark Twain is noted for saying, "Everybody talks about the weather but nobody does anything about it." Actually, Twain was quoting Charles Dudley Warner of Connecticut, which everyone knows has worse weather than Missouri.

Twain's wry brand of humor and tendency toward exaggeration are hallmarks of his home state. Missourians are masters of teasing. A mildly overweight man might be told that his table was gettin' a mite close to his belly, for example. An old hill farmer once turned a visiting social worker perfectly green by telling his daughter, "Git th' dishrag an' wipe that baby's nose! If they's one thing I cain't stand, it's nastiness!"

Missouri farmers have mastered similes, too. "Wild as a peach orchard boar," "hungrier'n a tick on a dead dog," "independent as a hog on ice," are a few that have delighted me. But the good, rich language is beginning to die out, replaced by the language of TV. How sad that kids today will grow up never knowing that a peach orchard boar got wild from eating fermented peach pits it found on the ground. Who will carry on with *bon mots* such as "If brains was dynamite, he couldn't blow his nose?" Or this fisherman's favorite: "A man's got to believe in something—I believe I'll go fishing."

There's probably more genuine stubbornness per acre of Missourians than can be found anywhere. We're not just phlegmatic, though. We simply want to be sure. Sometimes that requires care in explaining, as Missouri's motto, "The Show-Me State," implies.

"I come from a state that raises corn, cotton, cockleburs, and Democrats," said Congressman Willard Vandiver in 1899. "Frothy eloquence neither convinces me nor satisfies me. I'm from Missouri. You've got to show me."

Today, Missouri raises more soybeans than cotton and more Republicans than Democrats. But like the weather, that's also subject to change.

Like any writer who loves his state, I could blunt a hundred pens extolling its virtues. But there must be something left for you to discover and enjoy—and I have left plenty. The dying sun sends fingers of fire through the trees, creating coppery bands of light and dark. The shriek of the wind has sent the ghosts back to their rest. The old cabin that has borne such storms for a century will creak in protest but stand firm.

The clouds are boiling up thick and black. There's no more sun. It's time to go.

William Childress,
Boonville

Missouri mule, enduring symbol of a rugged state FRANK OBERLE

The Current River gushing through ancient Ozark rocks FRANK OBERLE

Greer Springs races toward Eleven Point River   FRANK OBERLE

Missouri, in different ways, occupies a unique position; unique in geography, population, history. In the North she is called the South. In the South she is called the North. In the east she is called the West. In the West she is called the East. She combines the good of all of these. She is almost the center of the United States, and may be considered the center of the world and of the universe.

Walter B. Stevens,
The Missourian

One billion-year-old boulders at Elephant Rocks State Park   GARRY D. McMICHAEL

Fallen leaves along Big Spring   GARRY D. McMICHAEL

Black River flowing through Johnson Shut-Ins GARRY D. McMICHAEL

The historic Alley Spring Mill near Eminence FRANK OBERLE

The Bollinger Mill near Burfordville standing on its original 1799 foundations FRANK OBERLE

Wood duck FRANK OBERLE

Two generations fishing for trout near Licking FRANK OBERLE

Carving paddles in the old way near the Current River FRANK OBERLE

Golden wheat bows its head to the sunset in northeast Missouri   FRANK OBERLE

Turning sorghum into molasses near Newtown FRANK OBERLE

*❝ Here's to the soil of Missouri;
her inexhaustible prairies of corn,
wheat and hay; her rolling expanses of
grass of bluest blood; her redlands
whose clay gives the peach its richness
of bloom and the apple its blush; her
broken bluffs whose thin-skinned fields
yield cotton; her bottom lands of
priceless timber wealth. ❞*

J. Breckenridge Ellis,
"Here's to Missouri"

Missouri farmer FRANK OBERLE

Picking cotton near Matthews, most northern cotton-growing area in the country   FRANK OBERLE

Shelled corn raining golden against the blue Missouri sky   FRANK OBERLE

Herefords grazing peacefully above a well-kept farm near Augusta   GARRY D. McMICHAEL

Cooling down on a hot day in Mexico (Missouri)   FRANK OBERLE

Thumping-good watermelons near Kennett   FRANK OBERLE

Picking the perfect pumpkin, St. Louis County   SHERRY LUBIC

Blue skies and gossamer clouds blessing the wheat crop BRUCE MATHEWS

Storm looming ominously over ripening wheat   FRANK OBERLE

" *The Ozark farmer may listen to the weather broadcast from Springfield or he may read it in the* Joplin Globe. *But he will check any forecast against reliable weather portents such as shooting stars, crowing roosters, croak of the rain crow, circle around the moon, and whether the sunset is clear or red.* "

Irving Dilliard,
I'm from Missouri

Peaches hanging heavy on branches near Campbell   FRANK OBERLE

Red delicious apples, tree ripened to perfection at the Stark Brothers Nursery, originators of the red and golden delicious strains   FRANK OBERLE

Spiked heads of milo sorghum near Warrenton   FRANK OBERLE

Tobacco field, Platte County   BOB BARRETT

Terraced rice fields in southeast Missouri   FRANK OBERLE

Soybeans, Missouri's top cash crop   FRANK OBERLE

Historic KCP&L Building dominating the Kansas City night   BOB BARRETT

The American Hereford Association monument in Kansas City   BOB BARRETT

Kansas City's Molley Trolley near the multi-colored fountains at Allis Plaza   BOB BARRETT

Jazz and blues, belted out Missouri style   FRANK OBERLE

> " *Scratch any Kansas Citian and he will tell you his town is 'a great place to live and a great place to raise your kids,' and if he means health and comfort and friendly neighbors he will be absolutely right.* "

Richard Rhodes,
The Inland Ground

Produce and flowers at the Kansas City Outdoor Market BRUCE MATHEWS

Tulips at Kansas City's Country Club Plaza   BOB BARRETT

Giraffe stretching for a peanut at the Kansas City Zoo   BRUCE MATHEWS

Parkway 600 Grill lighting up the Kansas City night   BRUCE MATHEWS

Water cascading in diamonds, blessing a couple in
downtown Kansas City   BRUCE MATHEWS

Kansas City's Crown Center, eighty-five acres of fun and shopping   JOHN AVERY

Kansas City fountain   BRUCE MATHEWS

Prairie coneflowers along the Current River   FRANK OBERLE

A quiet forest at Huzzah Wildlife Area near Steelville   FRANK OBERLE

Red-bellied woodpecker near Defiance BILL LUBIC

A buckeye bloom after a Missouri rainshower FRANK OBERLE

Whitetail buck sniffing for danger FRANK OBERLE

" *I can call back the solemn twilight and mystery of the deep woods, the earthy smells, the faint odors of the wild flowers, the sheen of rain-washed foliage, the rattling clatter of drops when the wind shook the trees, the far-off hammering of woodpeckers and the muffled drumming of wood grouse in the remoteness of the forest, the snapshot glimpses of disturbed wild creatures scurrying through the grass—I can call it back and make it as real as it ever was, and as blessed.* **"**

Mark Twain,
The Autobiography of Mark Twain

"The Scout" scanning the Missouri River valley
near Kansas City BRUCE MATHEWS

A bald eagle riding the wind above the Mississippi River
near Winfield FRANK OBERLE

Wine library at the Stone Hill Winery near Hermann BILL LUBIC

Aging properly in the Stone Hill cellars   SHERRY LUBIC

Grapes in the Augusta Wine District, first designated
winery district in the United States   FRANK OBERLE

Morning mist melting slowly in the rising sun near Weldon Spring   SHERRY LUBIC

66 *Ozark mists are like no others. They can shift, move, turn as the sun rises behind them, making swirling patterns that gradually lighten and finally disappear. Or you can top a rise and be in cold, clear glittering night, with stars cutting holes in the black sky above you while down in a swale or holler a white band of fog chalks out the middle of the trees, so the tops float like anchorless blimps.* *99*

William Childress,
Out of the Ozarks

Missouri oath: Everyone has to believe in something—I believe I'll go fishing   LEWIS PORTNOY

Jet skiing on Lake of the Ozarks   FRANK OBERLE

Summer school, Lake of the Ozarks style   CHET HANCHETT

Catching rays on a house boat   CHET HANCHETT

Knee boarding   TONY SCHANUEL

A bald eagle taking breakfast from the Mississippi River   FRANK OBERLE

Opening day for trout fishermen at Bennett Spring State Park near Lebanon   JOHN STEWART

Taking a trout in Ozark County   BILL LUBIC

Passion flower in full bloom FRANK OBERLE

Pink coneflower FRANK OBERLE

Yellow lady's slipper FRANK OBERLE

A wild iris in dew FRANK OBERLE

Field of crocus at the Missouri Botanical Gardens, St. Louis   FRANK OBERLE

Missouri hardwoods welcome the fall in radiant color   FRANK OBERLE

> " *I turned to see a gentle shower of gold raining down in the woods, hundreds of leaves leaving this life behind, as silent in their final going as they had been in their arrival a year ago. Even after the wind had died, not a breeze passing through the ranks of trees, the leaves still sifted down like molten snowflakes....* "

William Childress,
Out of the Ozarks

Canoes slipping down the Current River near Salem FRANK OBERLE

Sitting back along the Current River   FRANK OBERLE

Lazy, toe-dipping days in a handcrafted boat   FRANK OBERLE

Making brooms in Mutton Hollow near Branson   CHET HANCHETT

A quilter with her wares in Big Spring Park   FRANK OBERLE

Civil War parade recreated in St. Charles   FRANK OBERLE

Transportation from a different time
in historic St. Charles   FRANK OBERLE

Shoals, water, and bluff slicing the horizon near the KATY Trail on the Missouri River   FRANK OBERLE

❝ *I cannot describe the impression that the days of wandering in this river valley have made upon me.... The splendor of the forests is, especially during this month, beyond all description.* **❞**

Gottfried Duden,
Report on a Journey to the Western States
(and a Stay of Several Years Along the Missouri
During the Years 1824, '25, '26, and '27.)

Sail a'billow, crew at ease on an autumn day   FRANK OBERLE

KATY Trail, public hiking and biking path along the Missouri River   FRANK OBERLE

Missouri bluffs along the KATY Trail, known officially as the Missouri River State Trail   FRANK OBERLE

“ *There is about the Missouri landscape something intimate and known to me. While I drive around the curve of a country road, I seem to know what is going to be there, what the creek beds and the sycamores and walnuts lining them will look like, and what the color of the bluffs will be.* ”

Thomas Hart Benton,
An Artist in America

Red fox on the prowl BILL LUBIC

Pileated woodpecker BILL LUBIC

Prairie wildflowers in bloom at the Missouri Botanical Gardens   FRANK OBERLE

Fireworks and the Gateway Arch on the Fourth of July   FRANK OBERLE

Milles Fountain and Union Station at night in downtown St. Louis   FRANK OBERLE

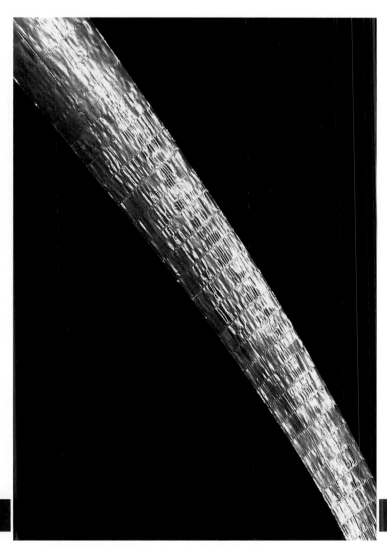

The stainless steel Gateway Arch glowing golden at night
FRANK OBERLE

> *The lights of St. Louis looked like a promised land to me.*
>
> Joseph Pulitzer

The restored Fox Theatre, built in 1929 as a movie theatre, now home to performing arts   FRANK OBERLE

Chandeliered Powell Hall, home to the St. Louis
Symphony Orchestra   TOM EBENHOH

The vaulted ceiling of the new St. Louis Cathedral   TOM EBENHOH

St. Louis Science Center FRANK OBERLE

Fun on a triceratops at the Science Center FRANK OBERLE

The St. Louis Art Museum   LEWIS PORTNOY

Family outing at Six Flags Over Mid-America   FRANK OBERLE

Waiting for the pitch at Busch Stadium, home to the St. Louis Cardinals   LEWIS PORTNOY

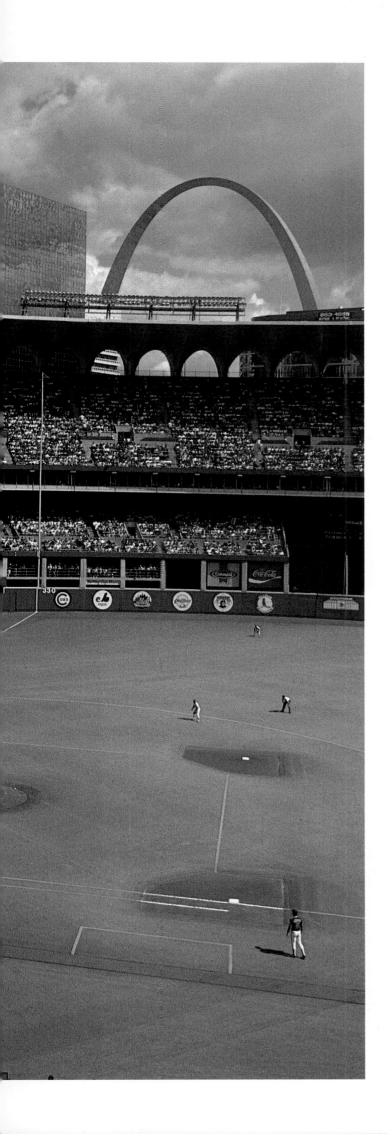

The flip, by St. Louis shortstop Ozzie Smith   J. B. FORBES

The Missouri Botanical Garden in St. Louis   FRANK OBERLE

Water lily at the Missouri Botanical Garden   LEWIS PORTNOY

Geese welcome visitors to Forest Park in downtown St. Louis   FRANK OBERLE

Fish frenzy at the Missouri Botanical Garden   GARRY D. McMICHAEL

President Harry Truman's home in Independence   BILL ENGEL

" *I always came back to Independence every chance I got because the people in Independence, the people in Missouri, had been responsible for sending me to Washington. And that's why when I ended up at the White House, after I had finished the job, I came back here. This is where I belong.* **"**

Harry S Truman,
Plain Speaking

"Give 'em hell" Harry's spirit remembered in Independence   BRUCE MATHEWS

Kansas City's Truman Sports Complex, mecca for Midwest sports fans   JOHN AVERY

Brewing vats at Anheuser-Busch, St. Louis   TOM TRACY

A Clydesdale stepping out at Grant's Farm, St. Louis   LEWIS PORTNOY

Anheuser-Busch offices at Christmas   LEWIS PORTNOY

A fern and columbine clinging to rocks on Spring Creek at Falling Spring near New Liberty, south of Winona FRANK OBERLE

Black-eyed susans FRANK OBERLE

Ox-eye daisies near Femme Osage   FRANK OBERLE

A great spangled fritillary butterfly on a
Canada thistle   BILL LUBIC

Mare and colt, part of the ever changing Missouri tapestry FRANK OBERLE

66 I never tire of the infinite variety of wildflowers and weeds, of pastures mellowed by the low, rich sun, of jade-colored grass covered with dew like diamonds in a rare tiara. If I were religious, I'd have a name for it. The ever changing tapestry of God. 99

William Childress,
Out of the Ozarks

Snow geese rising at dawn at Squaw Creek National Wildlife Refuge near Mound City   FRANK OBERLE

" *Then they were there. Up in the March blackness, two entwined skeins of snow and blue geese honking north, an undulating W-shaped configuration across the deep sky, white bellies glowing eerily with the reflected light from town, necks stretched northward. . .a new season.* **"**

William Least Heat Moon,
Blue Highways

Brick layers in St. Louis County DOUG MINER

Fabricating structural steel in Caruthersville   TOM EBENHOH

Drawing the lines in Clayton   FRANK OBERLE

Buyers and sellers betting on the futures at the Kansas City
Board of Trade   BRUCE MATHEWS

Sprinting bicycle racers at the V-P Fair, downtown St. Louis   LEWIS PORTNOY

Motocross racing near Bonneterre   FRANK OBERLE

Kodak Balloon Races near St. Charles   DOUG MINER

Taking a shower at the Keiner Plaza, St. Louis   FRANK OBERLE

Coxswain and crew of four pulling on Creve Coeur Lake, St. Louis County   FRANK OBERLE

The St. Francois River, the "Grand Canyon of the Midwest," eating a canoe   FRANK OBERLE

Crossing the Jack's Fork River, part of the Ozark National Scenic Riverway   FRANK OBERLE

The *Robert E. Lee*, moored near the Gateway Arch FRANK OBERLE

The mighty Missouri and Mississippi rivers converging above St. Louis   FRANK OBERLE

Golden Eagle ferry plying the waters between St. Charles County and Illinois
FRANK OBERLE

" . . . lifts up the cry, 's-t-e-a-m-b-o-a-t a-comin!' and the scene changes! The town drunkard stirs, the clerks wake up, a furious clatter of drays follows, every house and store pours out a human contribution, and all in a twinkling the dead town is alive and moving. . . . to a common center, the wharf. Assembled there, the people fasten their eyes upon the coming boat as upon a wonder they are seeing for the first time. "

Mark Twain

Hannibal on a Tom Sawyer kind of day   TOM EBENHOH

Tom and Becky look-alikes competing during Tom Sawyer Days in Hannibal   FRANK OBERLE

Spirit of St. Charles excursion boat   FRANK OBERLE

Meramec Caverns near Stanton   FRANK OBERLE

The Lily Pad Room in Onondaga Cave near Leasburg
FRANK OBERLE

Rail lines leading to the Gateway Arch   TONY SCHANUEL

Vetch flowering in a field near Washington   FRANK OBERLE

A stand of horsetail along the KATY Trail near Treloar FRANK CBERLE

Ice sculpture along Sandy Slough near Winfield   FRANK OBERLE

Hidden Valley ski area near Eureka   FRANK OBERLE

Swooshing over snowy hills in St. Charles   FRANK OBERLE

A common egret primping at its rookery on the Mississippi River near Elsberry   FRANK OBERLE

Feather plants like peacocks in the sun   TONY SCHANUEL

It's not easy being a baby great blue heron   FRANK OBERLE

Great blue herons perching on branch-like legs
FRANK OBERLE

"The Pony Express" statue in St. Joseph   FRANK OBERLE

Where they began in St. Joseph   CHET HANCHETT

“ There is no part of the western country that holds out greater attractions. .. ”

1804 immigrants' guide

Geese in a golden sunset   FRANK OBERLE

Commercial fishing on the Mississippi near Elsberry   FRANK OBERLE

Current undercutting a tree in the Ozarks   SAM MITCHELL

Raccoon stalking the Missouri woods   FRANK OBERLE

Gray squirrel fattened for winter   FRANK OBERLE

Screech owl at the Tyson Raptor Research Center
in Eureka   BOB BARRETT

A cottontail waiting out the Missouri winter   FRANK OBERLE

A Missouri meadow ablaze with wildflowers   FRANK OBERLE

Fire pink flowers, also known as catchfly for their ability to trap insects   FRANK OBERLE

Two adult bald eagles swapping stories along the Mississippi River near Clarksville   FRANK OBERLE

The main attraction in Big Oak Tree State Park near East Prairie FRANK OBERLE

" Comes that dreamy, tender feeling
For the woods, the hills, the grass,
And a sort of fervent wishing
For the days that now are past;
With a thought of swamp and river,
Where the cattle love to roam,
Comes that lingering kind of longing
For the old Missouri home. "

Missouri State University *Independent*,
Columbia, 1902

Sky and forest merging into infinity near Augusta   FRANK OBERLE

Tug and barges straining up the Mississippi River near St. Louis   C. MICHAEL HOUSKA

Painted turtles playing follow-the-leader   FRANK OBERLE

Keeping the channels open, Mississippi River near Foley   FRANK OBERLE

" The Mississippi is well worth reading about. It is not a commonplace river, but on the contrary is in all ways remarkable. "

Mark Twain

The first phase of a channel catfish dinner, along the Mississippi   FRANK OBERLE

Racing the sunset at Creve Coeur Park   FRANK OBERLE

Riding a historic carousel at Six Flags   FRANK OBERLE

> **❝** *Missouri . . . is the channel catfish and the small mouth black bass, the mallard, the squirrel and the rabbit. It is the red flash of the cardinal and the hoarse call of the crow. It is Jack in his pulpit and lace along the road for Queen Ann. It is the corn-cob pipe, square dancing and quilting bee; the country fair, potluck supper, school picnic and moonlight boatride.* **❞**

Irving Dilliard,
I'm from Missouri

Femme Osage, resting along a bend in the road   FRANK OBERLE

" ** *The pace of life here is as slow as the traffic on the winding, two-lane highways.* **"

William Childress,
Out of the Ozarks

Sharing lunch near Affton   TONY SCHANUEL

Lonesome stretch of the Missouri Ozark Highway
near Starkenburg   BOB BARRETT

An old shepherd and his mule working their way
home near Branson   CHET HANCHETT

they made it possible

Missouri on my Mind would have been impossible to produce without the creative and technical skills of Missouri photographer Frank Oberle and his company, Photographic Resources, a stock photo agency in St. Louis.

Frank Oberle is a nationally known nature and commercial photographer. His outdoor photography has appeared in several national magazines, including *Audubon*, while his images of business and industry, especially farming, have illustrated many publications.

To capture the many moods and faces of the Show Me State, Oberle traveled to all corners of the state in all seasons. He also enlisted the aid of several other well-known Missouri photographers.

From the rugged Ozarks to the mighty Mississippi, Missouri contains a breathtaking array of beautiful images, but transforming these images onto film requires more than just a camera. It takes an eye for composition, technical expertise, long hours of work, and the sheer determination to obtain a memorable shot rather than a mere snapshot.

Frank Oberle and the other photographers for *Missouri on my Mind* provided this extra skill and effort. They canoed, hiked, drove, waited, and watched to get the best possible images from all parts of the state.

To Frank Oberle and all the excellent photographers who assisted him, thank you.

Michael S. Sample,
Bill Schneider
Publishers, Falcon Press

Photographers in *Missouri on my Mind*

Frank Oberle
John Avery
Bob Barrett
Tom Ebenhoh
Bill Engel

J. B. Forbes
Chet Hanchett
C. Michael Houska
Bill Lubic
Sherry Lubic

Bruce Mathews
Garry D. McMichael
Doug Miner
Sam Mitchell
Lewis Portnoy

Tony Schanuel
John S. Stewart
Tom Tracy

All photographs were provided by Photographic Resources, St. Louis, Missouri.

acknowledgments

The publishers gratefully acknowledge the following sources:

Page 9 from *The Missourian* by Walter B. Stevens, included in *The Missouri Historical Review* 17, No. 2, January, 1923.

Page 18 from *Here's to Missouri* by J. Breckenridge Ellis, included in *Missouri* 1, No. 7, November, 1928.

Pages 23 and 115 from *I'm from Missouri* by Irving Dillard. Copyright © 1951 by Hastings House, Publishers, Inc.

Page 29 from *The Inland Ground* by Richard Rhodes. Copyright © 1970 by the author. Published by Atheneum.

Page 37 from *The Autobiography of Mark Twain*, edited by Charles Neider. Copyright © 1959 by The Mark Twain Company. Copyright © 1952 by Clara Clements Samossoud. Copyright © 1959 by Charles Neider. Published by Harper & Row, Publishers.

Pages 42, 51, 79, and 116 from *Out of the Ozarks* by William Childress. Copyright © 1987 by the author. Published by Southern Illinois University Press.

Page 55 from *Missouri Historical Review* 72, No. 3, April, 1978.

Page 56 from *Report on a Journey to the Western States of North America* by Gottfried Duden. Copyright © 1980 by The Curators of the University of Missouri. Published by The State Historical Society of Missouri and University of Missouri Press.

Page 58 from *An Artist in America* by Thomas Hart Benton. Copyright © 1983 by The Curators of the University of Missouri. Published by University of Missouri Press.

Page 63 from *Pulitzer* by W.A. Swanberg. Copyright © 1967 by the author. Published by Charles Scribner's Sons.

Page 72 from *Plain Speaking: An Oral Biography of Harry S Truman* by Merle Miller. Copyright © 1974 by the author. Published by Berkley Publishing Corporation.

Page 81 from *Blue Highways* by William Least Heat Moon. Copyright © 1982 by the author. Published by Little, Brown, and Company in association with The Atlantic Monthly Press.

Pages 89 and 101 from *The New Enchantment of America: Missouri* by Allan Carpenter. Copyright © 1966 by Childrens Press, Inc. Copyright © 1978 by Regensteiner Publishing Enterprises, Inc.

Page 110 from *Independent* 9, No. 16, January 29, 1902.

Page 113 from *Newsweek*, April 16, 1990.

About William Childress

William Childress, the author of the introduction to *Missouri on my Mind,* is a writer, photographer, poet, humorist, storyteller, musician, and backporch balladeer. A longtime Missouri resident now living in Boonville, Childress chronicles the state's people and places in a weekly column for the *St. Louis Post-Dispatch,* where his work has twice been nominated for the Pulitzer Prize. His articles also appear in a wide variety of national magazines, and he has written four books, including the highly acclaimed *Out of the Ozarks.* Equally adept with guitar, mandolin, and harmonica, Childress often entertains audiences throughout the state with his one-man program of music and verse. He also lectures at various colleges and writers workshops. His friends call him "Chilly."

Nature closing another day in Missouri   FRANK OBERLE